MAY 2008

BUG BOOKS

Bee

Karen Hartley and Chris Macro

Heinemann Library
Chicago, Illinois

Customer Service 888-454-2279
Visit our website at www.heinemannraintree.com

Designed by Ron Kamen, Michelle Lisseter, and Bridge Creative Services Limited
Illustrations by Alan Fraser at Pennant Illustration
Printed in China by South China Printing Company

10 09 08 07 06
10 9 8 7 6 5 4 3 2 1

New edition ISBN: 1-4034-8293-4 (hardcover)
                  1-4034-8306-X (paperback)

The Library of Congress has cataloged the first edition as follows:
Hartley, Karen, 1949-
      Bee/ Karen Hartley and Chris Macro.
         p. cm. -- (Bug books)
      Includes bibliographical references and index.
      Summary: A simple introduction to the physical characteristics, diet, life cycle, predators,
            habitat, and lifespan of bees.
      ISBN 1-57572-661-0 (lib. bdg.)
      1. Bees—Juvenile literature. [1. Bees.] I. Macro, Chris, 1940-. II. Title. III. Series.
QL565.2.H368 1998
      595.79'9—dc21   98-4858
                             CIP
                             AC

Acknowledgments
The author and publishers are grateful to the following for permission to reproduce photographs:
Bruce Coleman Ltd pp. 8 (J Brackenbury), 9 (J Cancalosi), 21 (J Shaw), 6, 12 (K Taylor); Corbis
p. 25 (PhotoCuisine); NHPA pp. 16 (N Callow), 4, 5, 13, 17, 18, 19, 20, 26 (S Dalton); Oxford
Scientific Films pp. 22, 29 (G Bernard), 15 (S Camazine), 24 (G Dew), 11 (B Osborne), 10
(R Packwood), 7, 14, 23, 27 (D Thompson); Premaphotos p. 28 (K Preston-Mafham).

Cover photograph reproduced with permission of Photolibrary.com/Oxford Scientific Films/Paulo
De Oliviera.

The publishers would like to thank Nancy Harris for her assistance in the preparation of this book.

Every effort has been made to contact copyright holders of any material reproduced in this
book. Any omissions will be rectified in subsequent printings if notice is given to the publisher.

The paper used to print this book comes from sustainable sources.

Some words are shown in bold, **like this**. You can find out what they mean
by looking in the glossary.

Contents

What Are Bees?

wing

legs

Bees are furry **insects**. They have six legs and two pairs of wings. They flap their wings so quickly they make a buzzing sound.

There are different types of bees. Mother bees are called queens. Male bees are called **drones**. There are also worker bees. They all have different jobs to do.

Bees have hairs on their bodies.
The hairs give the bees their brown
and yellow stripes.

Bees have two large eyes. They can see up, down, backwards, and forwards at the same time. They also have three small eyes. They have two **feelers** for touching and smelling.

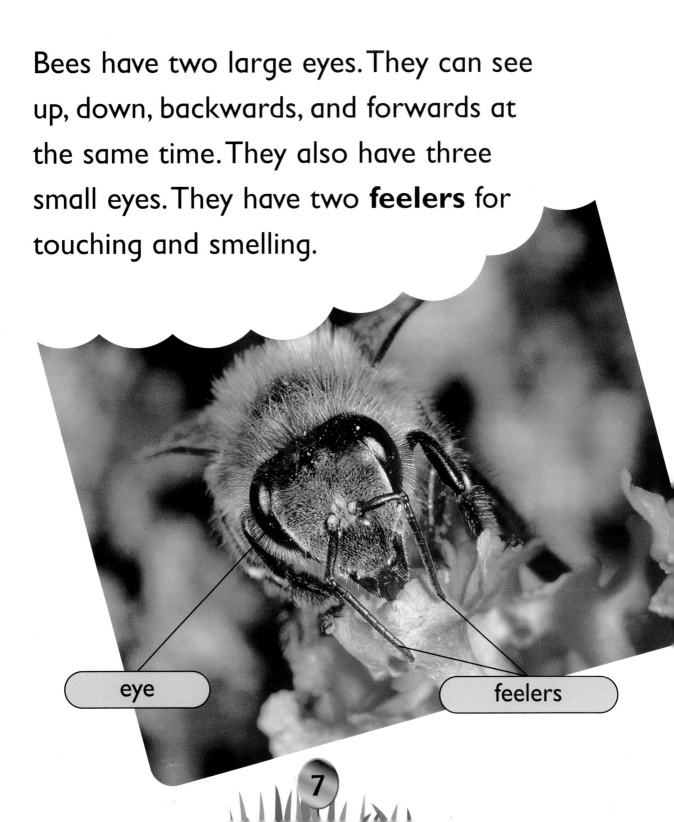

eye

feelers

How Big Are Bees?

Bumblebees are about the size of a grape. Honeybees are about the size of a peanut.

Queen bees are the biggest bees.
Workers are the smallest in the nest.
There is only one queen in each nest.

queen bee

Where Do Bees Live?

Bumblebees live together.
They live in a nest that sits in
long grass or underground.

Honeybees live together in a nest in a **hollow** tree or log. Sometimes people keep honeybees in a wooden hive.

How Are Bees Born?

In the spring, the queen bee **mates** with a male bee called a **drone**. She then lays her eggs in special places called cells. Cells are inside the nest.

After three days the babies **hatch**
out. They are called **larvae**. The
larvae are small and white. They
have no eyes, no legs, and no wings.

larva

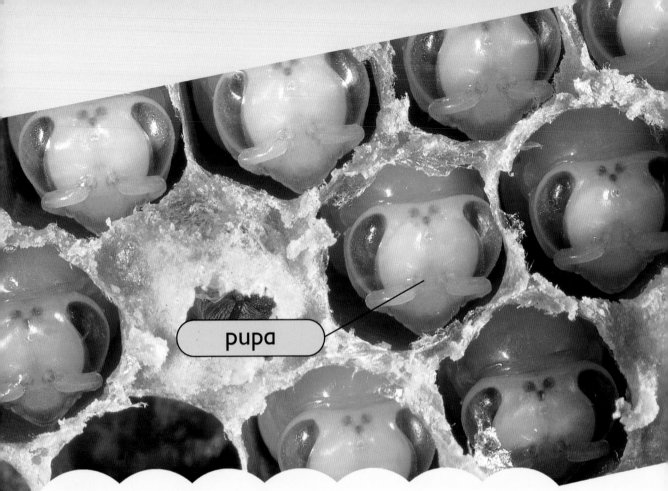

pupa

Soon, the **larvae** turn into young bees
called **pupae**. They begin to turn into
adult bees. After two weeks the new
bees push the tops of the cells off and
crawl out.

The young bees' bodies are very soft. They soon get harder. Most of the new bees are worker bees.

What Do Bees Eat?

pollen

tongue

Bees eat the **pollen** from flowers.
They bring juice called **nectar** from the
flowers to the nest. They make it into
honey, which they eat.

When **larvae** are in the cells they need to eat to grow. Worker bees feed them honey and pollen.

Which Animals Attack Bees?

Some birds eat bees. Queen and worker bees will sting if they are angry or frightened. Their stripes warn other animals to stay away.

Some worker bees guard the entrance of the nest. They fight bees from other nests if they come to steal honey.

How Do Honeybees Move?

Bees have strong wings. They can fly a long way to look for food. When it is hot, they fan their wings to keep the nest cool.

When bees land on a flower they crawl inside it to suck up the **nectar**. They also collect **pollen**. Their **feelers** help them to smell and taste.

How Long Do Bees Live?

Queen bees live for up to six or seven years. Most of the bees stay in their nest through the winter. The worker bees will die during the next summer.

Worker bees push the male **drones** out of the nest in the fall and keep them from coming back in. The drones die because they have no food to eat.

What Do Honeybees Do?

When there are too many bees in a nest, the queen takes a big group called a **swarm** to find a new nest. Another bee becomes the queen in the old nest.

24

Gardeners like worker bees because they take **pollen** from flower to flower. This makes new seeds, so new flowers grow. Many people also like to eat the honey that bees make.

How Are Bees Special?

Bees have long hairs on their back legs that work like baskets. They put **pollen** from flowers into the baskets. Their legs look like yellow balloons.

26

Bees do a special dance to show
other bees where there are lots
of flowers.

Thinking About Bees

Why are bees so busy?

What jobs do worker bees do?

Would you like to be a male **drone**?

This person is collecting honey from the beehive. Why do you think beekeepers wear gloves and a veil? Why do they puff smoke at the bees?

Bug Map

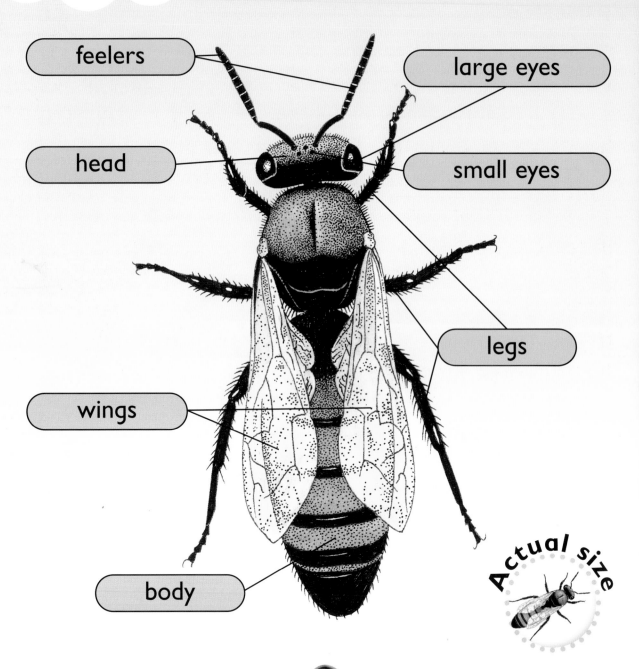

feelers

large eyes

head

small eyes

legs

wings

body

Actual size

Glossary

drone male bee

feelers two long narrow tubes that stick out from the head of an insect. They may be used to feel, smell, or even hear.

hatch to come out of an egg

hollow a hollow tree is usually a dead tree and the trunk is empty inside

insect small creature with six legs

larva (more than one = larvae) the baby that hatches from an egg

mate male and female bees mate to make baby bees

nectar sweet juice inside flowers

pollen golden dust inside flowers

pupa (more than one = pupae) older larva

swarm hundreds of bees all flying together to find a new nest

Index

More Books to Read

Barraclough, Sue. *Bees.* Chicago: Raintree, 2005.